Meditate Like Your Cat

A simple guide to entering a blissful state of consciousness

AF583095

Buster M. Studebaker

©2023 Alden Studebaker
https://aldenstudebaker.com
ISBN: 9798373988735

https://aldenstudebaker.com

Cover design: Jennifer Studebaker

No part of this book may be reproduced, stored in a retrieval system, or transmitted by any means without the written permission of the author.

Dedication

This book is dedicated to people who are owned by cats.

Acknowledgments

Donna Studebaker, my wife, who continues to support me as my editor-in-chief and loving inspiration.

Jennifer Studebaker, for her expert copy editing, creation of the front cover, and web promotion.

Dani Studebaker, for many of the photos in this book.

Buster, our cat, who inspired me to write this little book.

"No, hooman, I dictated this book to you!"

Foreword

I began meditating in earnest after I was introduced to the work of Master Subramuniya by my father's business partner, A. Roy Horn. He had come to Honolulu in 1971 to study with Subramuniya, a teacher who had an ashram on the Island of Kau'ai. A. Roy was an avid meditator. He would begin his sessions each morning that went on for a couple of hours, often thwarting my father's "let's get working now" approach to business. The office was in an apartment building on Kalakaua Avenue that also served as Roy's domicile. Through A. Roy I began reading Subramuniya's books and was introduced to him once when he was in town.

A year later my mother dragged me kicking and screaming to the Unity church on Diamond Head Circle telling me that I would like the message. Fifteen-year olds generally don't like being hauled to church by their parents. Surprisingly, Rev. Stan Hampson's message resonated with me, and soon afterward the Youth of Unity (Y.O.U) teenage group invited me to their meetings.

Unity people are meditators, or at least they're doing their best to meditate. We meditated in the church service and in group meetings. It was the way to re-center one's self, to "know the truth, and the truth will set you free." (John 8:32)

Fifty years later I continue to apply myself in meditation, but now I do it with the help of a "professional," as you'll discover in the essays presented in this little book.

Alden Studebaker (Buster's hooman)
Winter 2022-23

Table of Contents

I'm Too Busy

Hoomans, that's what we cats call you. As a grouping of sentient beings we find you to be the most industrious on the planet, except for the dung beetle. Why are you too busy to meditate? Because you're too damn busy! You are doing way more than you need. Trust me, I watch you all the time. Even retired hoomans are busier than when they had paying jobs.

Please listen to me when I say: Being busy is not your goal in life. It's okay to have things to do. I like to lick myself pretty much every day, hence all the hairballs I cough up that you dispose of on my behalf. But, I'm not busy. I engage in enough activity to be a responsible member of my species on our planet. I eat, I barf, I sleep, and repeat. Pretty normal. Why can't you just do what is correct for your species?

Being too busy is strictly optional. If you don't want to be busy stop yourself and relax a little. It's not that hard. Trust me. I'm a professional when it comes to relaxing, chilling, and, of course, meditating. It's because I'm not busy like you always seem to be. I'm totally okay with who I am. I don't have to prove myself to anybody or meet their expectations of what a cat should be. I don't care. You shouldn't care either.

Next time you have the urge to be busy (probably about five seconds from now) just tell the *busy idea* that you don't care one whit about what it thinks you should be doing. Shake your head from side to side when you're talking to the *busy idea.* And, keep it up. Tell it that whether you're busy or not busy is none of its blankety-blank business! Yeah, you can do it! I have faith in you, hooman. We'll make a meditator out of you yet.

I know from whence I speak. My primary hooman is a minister, and there's isn't a bigger black hole of a job than being a member of the clergy. Their inbox is always full. He's always in motion. He's busy.

He teaches meditation, leads meditation, but his meditation practice is…sporadic. He needs to stop all the busyness more often and sit his butt down and meditate.

He could meditate like his cat. He could just close his eyes, and smile a little. I smile at everything. That's what I look like I'm doing with my eyes shut. When you meditate, start with a smile. Do it! If you want to experience bliss, put on the face of bliss!

You see, when you're smiling you're not busy. Busy people rarely smile. Meditative people smile more. You need to smile more…to counteract the busy inclinations that will inevitably pop up.

Your Torment

You hoomans unnecessarily torture yourselves with how you approach life. Why? Not enough meditation. You let the outer world and all of its "demands" suck your energy dry. Why do you do that to yourselves? I don't get it. You let other people's expectations jerk you around. I don't. You tell me to do something I take it under consideration and then ignore your request. It's the decent thing to do. Then I go back to what I want to do. Napping, mostly.

Nothing in your life is more important than your time sitting in the Silence. Yogis and the early metaphysicians made meditation a priority. You apparently don't. You fit it into to your Google calendar, or whatever that thing is in your smartphone. My hooman at least uses a good ole fashioned paper calendar with a pencil to make corrections. But, he's a "meditation fitter." He looks for little windows of time to sit quietly, like when I get him up at 4:00 a.m. to sit with me on the couch. He's pretty good about that, and he's learned to fill my food dish before he sits down to meditate. He would not be able to meditate if he didn't. Trust me, I would make sure of it. Never forget, I own him, not the other way around. Nobody owns a cat.

Hoomans are tormented by many things, especially what they perceive others expect of them. I just shake my head when I see them trying to listen to these ideas floating around in their noggins. Stuff like, "I better do this or so-

and-so will think I'm not perfect." Perfect?! Hooman, you're not perfect. I'm perfect, or should we say, "purrfect." Haha! Bad joke.

I don't give a rat's posterior what hoomans, other cats, or dogs think of me and my accomplishments, and I certainly don't let it disturb my meditation time. You must learn to discipline yourself, to let the chatter box of "have-tos" and "shoulds" just drift away. Otherwise, you'll be stuck, tormented by these faux priorities. Your priority is meditation. Remember, that's why you sat down in a comfortable, supportive chair, closed your eyes, breathed deeply and rhythmically, and focused your awareness inward. You're not sitting there to entertain unwelcome guests. All they do is eat everything in the fridge, dominate the TV remote, and make themselves at home. (I've seen the SNL skit with John Belushi)

Please do not let these guys set up shop in your head. They are the mosquitos of consciousness. I ignore them. You can too. The "have-tos" and "shoulds" will not take you where you want to go, and after a while you forget why you sat down in the first place. Wake up and say to yourself, "Dang, what am I doing? Get outah here!" And as if by magic, the errant, distracting, nagging thoughts that so dominated the arena of your mind will take a hike and you can return to deep, rhythmic breathing.

Put It Down

Yeah, put it down. You know what I mean. It's about 3″ wide and 6″ long (7cm x 15cm for those outside the United States). Oh, and it's very thin, less than half an inch. You're either holding it in your hand, got it in your pocket, or are reading this book on it. Put it down. Now!!!

That's better. Smartphones are by far the greatest impediment to successful meditation. Don't start crying. Boo-hoo! If you want to meditate like me you're going to have to put it down. The reason that I'm successful at meditating is because I don't have a mobile phone. Yeah. You're thinking, "How can you, Buster M. Studebaker, navigate the complexities of modern life without one?" My answer: "No problemo!"

I'm a cat. I don't require constant connection, stimulation, or the obsession with other people's opinions on the latest thing going on in the world of…whatever. Yeah, I know about the special smartphone apps that are supposed to help you meditate. As good as they might be, they are no substitute for the actual experience of meditation.

The lure of an electronic device is compelling but not overwhelming. You must learn to consciously cut the umbilical cord between you and your phone if you want to meditate. So, put it down. Don't touch it! Don't look at it! Put it on silent mode. Better yet, turn it off and put it in another room, out of sight. You're apprehensive about doing that, aren't you? It's like the Harry Nilsson song from the 70s, "I can't live if living is without you…" Let me ask you, how did you live before you had one? Did you treat your flip phone or brick phone with the same reverence?

Put it down! Facebook, Instagram, YouTube, TikTok, Twitter, and all the other internet platforms will survive the next twenty minutes without your attention. I swear, it's true! Oh, you hoomans. You are a strange bunch of sentient beings.

Let me put this in algebraic language for you:

Smartphone = No meditation.

No smartphone = Meditation is likely.

Put it down, or I will come to your house and remove it myself. I can do that. Ask my hooman if you don't believe me. I have some serious claws and will swat that puppy out of your hand if you lean over to pick it up. So, put it down. Just put it down.

There Is No Hurry

Once you phone is secured, you're breathing correctly, and not staring at your widescreen TV (yeah, turn that off too!), it's time to go a little bit deeper.

This isn't a race. Or as they used to say, there is no fire. Enter meditation gracefully. It's a mellow experience. If you rush it you'll fail. This will be challenging for Type A hoomans. You're all about getting stuff done. There is no "done" in meditation. There are no deadlines, no to-do lists, no demanding tyrannical bosses.

It's just you and yourself. We'll talk about God later.

Don't make your twenty minutes of contemplative bliss a quarter-mile drag race. There's no prize for the fastest meditator. The Bible says, "So the last shall be first, and the first last."(Matthew 20:16, KJV) I'll bet that passage never made any sense to you. I'm taking this out of context, but this passage specifically pertains to the meditator. You need to approach meditation like you *want to come in last*.

Meditation is not about being a stellar multi-tasker. It's a very singular task experience (dare we even use the word "task"). Multi-taskers are always in constant motion, working from one thing to another to another, and then back to again. Give this up, hooman! There are no brownie points or gold stars for multi-tasking in meditation. You're there to sit quietly, eyes closed, breathing evenly and chillin'. Think you can do that?

I know how you feel guilty when you're not doing something productive, something that you can tangibly measure. But, if you're going to be able to meditate like I do, a cat, you have to abandon that emotional pattern. Guilt has no place in meditation. Nobody is grading you. Nobody is watching you. Nobody cares. I don't care if I'm not doing something and you shouldn't either. Learn to be more like me.

Here are some affirmations you can use to slow down your hooman mental activity. I don't use them because, I'm a cat and I don't need tools to experience meditation. I do it naturally. But, I know how much you hoomans need guides and implements to achieve your goals:

RELAX.
THERE IS NO HURRY.
THERE IS NO RACE.
THERE IS NO TROPHY FOR FIRST PLACE.
THE FIRST SHALL BE LAST AND THE LAST SHALL BE FIRST. (that's for the Bible folks)

Just Breathe

Most hoomans are unaware that they're breathing. They simply breathe without regard for the importance of their breath. They breathe unconsciously. For a moment, let your awareness rest on your breath. Become aware of the air flowing through your nostrils, inhale, exhale, and repeat. This is how to begin meditation. You would think that you must close your eyes first, but I suggest you start with breath awareness then close your eyes. This is the signal to your body that you're going to be meditating.

Meditation is impossible if your breath is hurried, strained, or constricted. Why? As your breath goes so goes your awareness.

Look at me. I'm a fantastic breather. Just watch me. I take in nice, even breaths all the time. Occasionally, this is interrupted by the sound of a can opener or plastic package, but on the whole I'm the best relaxed breather on planet earth. How do I do this, you may ask? Practice. Uh-oh, there's that word!

Let your breath move the same distance in and out. It's not that hard. All of us cats across the world are mentors for your breathing practice. Imagine that you are one of us, sitting calmly, breathing without effort yet easily with no anxiety. That's it! You've got this! We're proud of you! We all are. Well, maybe not. We're cats.

Hooman, it's called diaphragmatic breathing. Look at me, at my belly! See it? It goes up and down, up and down. I'm not hyperventilating. These are even breaths without stress or strain. Do you think you can manage this simple exercise?

Focus, A Little

Once you're smiling, chillin', breathing nicely, and have closed your eyes, it's time to direct your sense of individual awareness in a specific direction. Begin by first becoming aware of your bodily sensations. Many think meditation is an escape from the body, the flesh, the corporeal. Not true. In order to transcend the physical world you must come to terms with it or it will prevent you from experiencing meditation.

So, tune in to your body. If you sense something out of the ordinary such as pain, an itch, or perhaps tiredness, acknowledge it. Be okay with what you discover and continue to relax. If you must, scratch that itch! I do it all the time. Sometimes I scratch my fur right off if it's a real prickly one.

Most hoomans don't live much in their bodies. Unless they exercise regularly, they live 90% of their lives in their minds. You know you do. Your awareness nearly constantly bounces around inside your head like a rubber ball. Boom-boom-boom! You jump from one thought to another to another, and so on.

Take a moment to observe the movement of your awareness through the mind. As this is unfolding identify the thoughts by naming what they are. Think of it like walking into a living room. There's a sofa in the middle, an armchair on the left, and a lamp on the right.

What's in your mental living room? If it's fear of failing at meditation then say, "There's my thought of failing at meditation." If it's about something you forgot to pick up at the grocery store then say, "There's my thought of forgetting what to buy at the store." Keep going. Mentally, point at these thoughts and call them for what they are.

You might feel a little stupid doing this. What the heck am I doing pointing at thoughts and naming them like a child looking at a video of farm animals? You are a child, a child at meditating. So, start where you find yourself within the echo chamber of your mind with the bouncing rubber ball.

As you name your thoughts as if they were things (and they are things just as much as your clothing, your phone, your eyeglasses) you'll start to develop inner perspective. You'll begin to separate your individual identity from your thoughts and in time you'll identify more with the pure awareness that touches these thoughts. This will help to reduce the mental frenzy that is so endemic in hooman consciousness and allow you to focus inwardly, a little bit.

The energy that was tied up in thought obsession will return back to you, to your sense of individual awareness, which is pure energy. Let it rest in your heart region and smile. Allow the experience to intensify, not in a "I'm gonna make this happen!" approach, but as a natural flow of your meditation practice.

It's All Around You

You're not here to find God. You're already in God, or whatever you call the Prime Source. Wherever you are, you are in God, and God is in you. It's all around you. This is called omnipresence. There's nothing you can do to strive for it, go toward it, or at it because, my dear hooman, you're in it!

I know you hoomans like to make extra trouble for yourselves all of the time. For some odd reason, that us cats do not understand, you seem to impede your quest for enlightenment by putting roadblocks in the way. For instance, you took Jesus, a carpenter and teacher from Galilee, and made him practically God. You wrote in your Bible that one can only experience God if you believe in Jesus. Holy crap! Sorry Bible literalists, but it's just not true.

Jesus didn't write this, nor did he likely say it. If you read the rest of your Gospels you'll discover that he was all about God accessibility. He called God, Father and Daddy. Those are intimate, personal words. Jesus doesn't care about your putting him on a pedestal, he just wants you to DO THIS: "But you, when you pray, go into your room, and when you have shut your door, pray to your Father who is in the secret place; and your Father who sees in secret will reward you openly." (Matthew 6:6).

The majority of meditation masters have been Hindus and Buddhists. Westerners, who I likely assume most of you are since this book is written in English, have looked to these religions for guidance on meditation practice. They don't require accepting any one person as your savior in order to experience God.

You don't need an intermediary to escort you into the presence of God. Again, there is no specific religious ritual you must perform, like an entrance fee into the *Disneyland of Spiritual Awareness*. Remember, you're in God right now. You're freakin' swimming in it! So, please do me this favor. Jettison all of the mental and emotional blocks you've created or accepted that say "I must do this to know God." They are false gods.

Cats since time immemorial have known this truth. We are among the titans of knowing the truth. We don't let anybody tell us some line of bull hockey that we're not among the chosen because of some line in a book, even a holy one. Remember, all books were written by hoomans, hoomans with a purpose. Truth is sometimes found in books, but it is not experienced in books, even this one you're reading. It's about experience, the direct apprehension of a reality. When you feel and sense a something within you and around you that is more rarefied, more expansive than you have ever experienced in your life, then you're aware and are swimming in it.

Beyond The Circumference

You hoomans live on the edge. I don't mean the usual definitions of that phrase. Only a very small number of you are daredevils, or push the envelope of your experience all that much. I mean, the edge of the mind. This is why you suck at meditation.

The edge, or circumference of the mind, is the realm of the physical, material world. You're obsessed with it. This is not about the half-hour a day many of you engage in fitness exercise. This is about your awareness being constantly overwhelmed with concerns, desires, and plans that solely involve your material existence.

Hey, I'm not putting down the physical world. I do expect you to fill my food dish several times a day, fill up my water dispenser, and clean my litter box. And…treats are always welcome. But, you hoomans are hooked into circumference thinking.

Even when you supposedly go to sleep your minds are locked into material issues. I hear you talk to each other with the lights out until the wee hours. As a cat, I find this quite annoying since I'm doing my best to get in my seventeen hours per day of sleep.

Meditation is not experienced through circumference thinking. If that's your approach, it is in vain. We must let go of the circumference of consciousness and allow ourselves to experience what lies beyond it. It is the rarified place in consciousness that is present within you. It's a consciousness that is expansive, all-encompassing, and self-sustaining. It is vaster than the physical universe. It is what lies behind physical existence, and the deeper you go into it, the more you realize what a fool you've been for believing that the outer world is all there is.

No Expectations

Our approach to meditation must be free of expectations or objectives. If you hold these you'll be disappointed. Meditation is the flow of energy, what you call "spirit," and that flows where it may, not according to a set of quantifiable goals. Expect nothing. Better yet, just delete expectation from your vocabulary.

When I close my eyes to meditate I don't plan. I just relax and let it 'er rip! It doesn't take me long to enter meditation because I don't have to encounter all of my reasons, intentions, and motivations for meditating. I just do it and I'm there. Check out the front cover, or leaf through the photos in this book. Cats are trying to teach you, hooman! They've been there all along, meditating and demonstrating frequently the best methods.

We transcend expectations. Whatever our experience is we accept it. If we're just relieving the stress of not getting treats when we want them, that's okay. If we're tuning out whatever show you're watching on TV, that's okay too. If we experience total oneness with the Universe, we're fine with that. No expectations mean no disappointments. Disappointments can lead to you dropping off the meditation road and resuming non-meditative hooman habit patterns. That's not so good.

So, close your eyes, take in a couple of breaths, become aware of the thoughts sitting on the furniture of your inner living room, and relax. See what happens. Do this daily. It's not gonna to hurt. It's free. I have faith you can do it.

Live Here Now

There is only one time, right now. The past is a present moment look at what has been. The future is a present moment look at what might happen. It's all happening right now.

Cats live in the present moment. You should too since it is reality! "Keep it real, hooman!" Meditation happens in the present moment. Yes, there are moments that unfold from the present moment, but it's still the present moment.

When cats are meditating they are fully engaged in the present moment. There's not a hint of digression from the moment. We revel in the moment. Look at how easy we forget the so called wrong things we do when our hoomans yell at us to stop. Toppling a Christmas tree? Hah! We do it and then we're off to the next fun thing to do, like attacking all the decorations lying on the floor.

We're not stuck in the past; not stuck in the future. For me, there is only now. You hoomans must learn to extricate yourselves from the illusion of the past or future if you want to experience meditation. Understanding history is a helpful thing in knowing what to do differently. Having plans and goals for the future keep you moving forward, but it's not where you really live. It's in the present where you experience meditation.

Be Like Me

I've written this book to help you, hooman. If you are owned by a cat, meditate like it. If you're not, find a cat and let it teach you.

When you hear us purring, that's the equivalent of your using the mantra, OM, to settle down the chatter of your mind.

Hoomans say we're aloof and disengaged from others. This is an incorrect characterization. We engage in selective awareness and selective response. This is not being aloof. It's what successful and experienced meditators do. We're not so caught up in the rat race of life that we're completely cut off from the inner life. We approach life with discretion. We observe. We are not easily swayed by hype. We're poised.

Don't envy us, be like us. We were placed on this earth to be your life coaches, and what's more life enhancing than becoming a meditator? You can meditate like your cat.

Further Reading

Hooman, I have listed only these books that you can easily buy from Amazon. There are many more, of course, but these will get you started.

The Cloud of Unknowing, 14th c. Anonymous

An Easy Guide to Meditation, Roy Eugene Davis

Finding Grace at the Center, Thomas Keating, M. Basil Pennington, Thomas Clarke

Other Books by Alden Studebaker

Wisdom for a Lifetime in the 21st Century

How to Get the Bible Off the Shelf and Into Your Hands

Wisdom for a Lifetime was first published in 1998 by Unity Books and became the go-to Bible handbook for students throughout the New Thought world with over 13,000 copies sold. Its purpose is to empower progressive spiritual seekers with the tools and encouragement to do their own relevant interpretations of biblical stories and passages. The book offers practical, occasionally humorous, and valuable information about how to study the Bible including: Understanding the evolution of the English Bible and how to select a Bible. This second edition includes updates on the use of electronic tools that make Bible study an easier and friendlier process.

The Grid

The Grid is a novel that explores power on many levels. These include physical, electrical, political, economic, and spiritual. The setting for *The Grid* is the electric power business. Hank Hudson is an overworked mechanical engineer from a Midwest utility. Natasha Shakhova is a beautiful Russian nuclear power plant director. Dieter Schmidt is the ruthless CEO of Energia, an international energy company. Energia has developed an unconventional way of producing electrical energy, one that doesn't use fuel, nor creates environmentally destructive pollution. What's so sinister is that Energia is suppressing this discovery. Hank and Natasha meet at an energy conference in Strasbourg, France, and unsuspectingly become engaged in an urgent mission to bring this new technology into safe hands. Will they prevail, or will Energia's security henchmen prevent them from succeeding? The implications for the world are staggering.

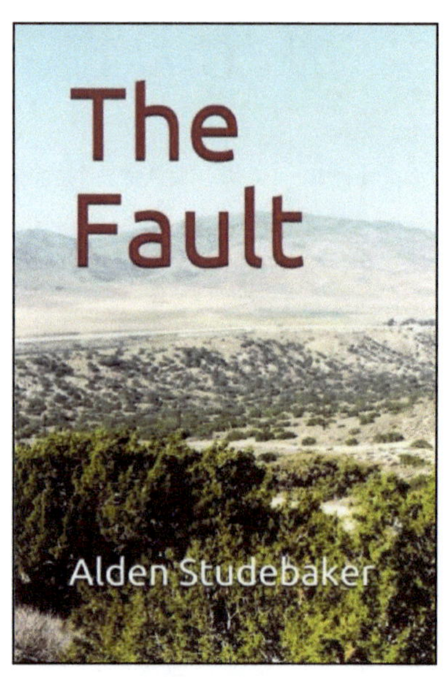

The Fault

The Fault is a novel set in the world of seismology. While millions of Angelenos go about their daily lives unaware of the seismological danger that lurks beneath, Cal Stover, a dedicated geologist from US Geological Survey, uncovers the threat that could trigger disaster for all. When he is found murdered near a gold mine next to the San Andreas Fault, the police suspect a connection between the mine and his untimely death. Cal's friend and colleague, Alex Demurjian, a local geology professor, and Kiraz Karahan, an alluring lecturer from Istanbul, are unexpectedly thrown together. Through an intuitive sensitivity, she discovers when "the fault" will slip. Can they save Greater Los Angeles from the impending peril? Will Cal's killer be caught? Along the way Alex and Kiraz experience not only the reconciliation of their ancestral past, but discover one another.

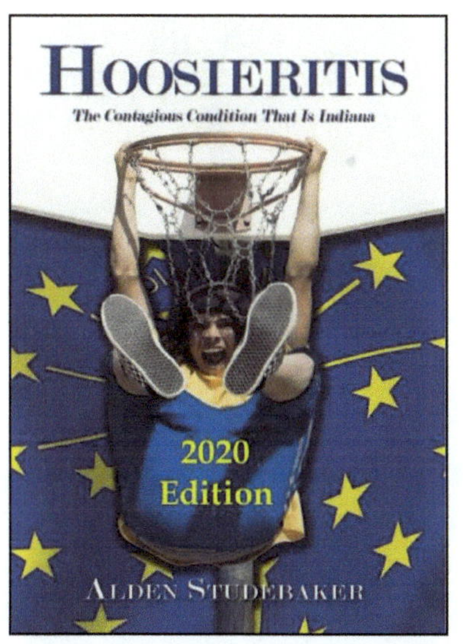

Hoosieritis – The Contagious Condition That Is Indiana

Is everyone in Indiana afflicted with an incurable disease? That's what author, Alden Studebaker, would have you believe in his book *Hoosieritis: The Contagious Condition that is Indiana.* A native son of Indiana, Studebaker takes the reader on an anecdotal, farcical journey through the Hoosier State pointing out the distinctive ways the enigmatic disease of Hoosieritis impacts the lives of Indiana residents. The book is often irreverent, poking fun at Hoosier institutions, traditions, and peculiarities by presenting selected nonsensical facts about Indiana's culture, history, people, and values. Its intent is to provoke robust conversations among Hoosiers about their home state, and spawn fresh, new observations of the concocted contagion.

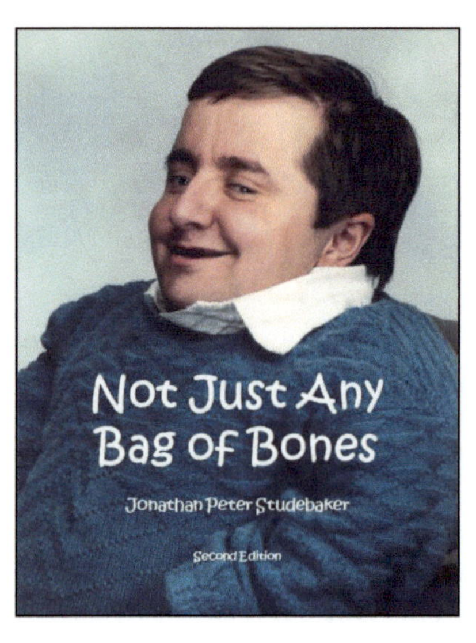

Not Just Any Bag of Bones (editor)

Not Just Any Bag of Bones is more than just an autobiography; it's a testament to the indomitable spirit that was Jonathan Peter Studebaker. Throughout his life, Jonathan wanted to be a normal human being and not just another person stuck in a wheelchair. Although he never played competitive sports, Jonathan was as much an athlete as any who wore a jersey. Although he never realized his dream to become an NFL coach, he came darn close. You will learn firsthand what it's like to be physically disabled and dependent on others for the living of your life. You will feel the pain people with severe disabilities go through on a daily basis. You will see through the eyes of someone who wanted access to everything able-bodied people simply take for granted. You will be forced to get off whatever pity pot you may be sitting on and begin to live your own life to the fullest.

About the Author

Alden Studebaker is an Indiana native, and spent his early childhood years living along the shore of Lake Michigan in the village of Dune Acres. At age ten his family moved to Honolulu, Hawaii. He has a BA degree in religion from Western Michigan University and was ordained as a Unity minister in 1984.

For further information:
https://aldenstudebaker.com

www.ingramcontent.com/pod-product-compliance
Lightning Source LLC
LaVergne TN
LVHW021307160826
845679LV00001B/246

* 9 7 9 8 3 7 3 9 8 8 7 3 5 *